Morris, Sarah
Grief and h
with it

GRIEF
AND HOW TO LIVE WITH IT

GRIEF AND HOW TO LIVE WITH IT

SARAH MORRIS

THE FAMILY INSPIRATIONAL LIBRARY

Grosset & Dunlap
A National General Company
Publishers *New York*

Library of Congress Catalog Card Number: 70-158744
ISBN: 0-448-01640-0
Published simultaneously in Canada
Printed in the United States of America

Contents

1
Introduction

SOME YEARS AGO MY HUSBAND DIED. Had I known then what I know now about the experience of grief, I would have mourned, of course, but I would have been aware of what was happening to me. I would have known how to handle my bewildering emotions, what to expect from other people, and—strangely enough—what to expect from myself. Knowing something about these three points would have provided me with a pattern to follow and would have kept me from floundering through a new and tragic experience.

First grief is usually very private. People are not aware of others' reactions to it. Every bereaved person—suddenly and alone—enters the unfamiliar, frightening world of grief. They are defenseless, these newly bereaved.

My husband was the Director of the University Theatre. We both taught at a university, he in Speech, I in English. Although our marriage was a second one for both of us and one of middle age, it was a fulfillment for each of us. After six years it ended suddenly and tragically in his death. The first thought that crossed my mind on hearing of his death was, "Now there are so many funny things that never will be said."

After he died I was confused, desperate, completely without direction. I felt a turmoil of emotions that I did not understand. I wondered where I could turn to discover what was happening to me and how to handle the terrible feelings that overwhelmed me, for I had changed into a someone I did not even recognize as myself.

Having studied and worked several years in counseling and personnel, I had been oriented to psychological explanations. I therefore looked to psychology for the special insight that it offers those who grieve. I felt I might find help by reading what others had to say about grief. Almost frantically I went to the library to look through subject guides to books—then those for magazines—for the past year, for the past two years, and finally I checked back for ten years. I found many articles describing heartbreaking personal grief, but no real answers to my problem. Other people, obviously, were crying out for the same help that I needed.

There are applied psychologies in other areas of human need, for instance, the psychology of adolescence. But why was there nothing on the psychology of grief? A few articles, each discussing an individual adolescent, could not give parents and teachers solid help in understanding teenagers. Nor could a few case histories of people in grief give me an understanding of the psychology of grief. But there was nothing else.

Finally I found a useful article on grief in a psychiatric journal. I have a doctor's degree in psychology and counseling, and this made it possible for me to wade through its technical terms. I began to get some ideas on what I was looking for. This article contained a bibliography, and I sent for reprints of some of its articles from a medical library. This led to obtaining other articles and finally I worked out what I needed on the psychology of grief. There *was* specialized information on the subject; the basic ideas were repeated over and over in articles on psychiatry—articles that were certainly not easily available to the average reader. Furthermore, the psychiatrists who wrote them naturally emphasized the abnormal aspects of grief, but the pattern for "uncomplicated" grief emerged clearly from what they said. Through this research I learned how to deal with my new emotions in ways that were better—much better—than the futile efforts I had been making.

But why should the psychology of grief be buried in *psychiatric sources?* Grief is a universal experience. Its problems come as surely to each person as do the problems of any other period of strain in a normal life span, and the help that psychology can give people in grief should not be kept behind psychiatrists' doors. It should be readily available to those who need it.

According to two authorities, the information on adjustment to grief is "scanty," for this subject has been "so little studied." No wonder I had difficulty in finding what I needed if it was difficult to find even in technical sources.

By talking with others in grief, I learned that they, too, suffered because they made the same kinds of mistakes that I had. I knew that they could get as much help as I did from the ideas or principles that resulted from my search. Hence this book: it is meant to give the individual who grieves some insight into ways of handling his feelings, and it can also help by evaluating the well-meaning but sometimes poor advice so generously given and so eagerly sought at the time of a death.

This book is intended to help us, the living, to work through our grief to the time when we can build a new life for ourselves. The time it takes to do this varies greatly. Grief may uncover problems that some people were not aware of in generally satisfactory lives, and such psychological problems may make it impossible for some to face the pain of resolving grief. Whatever the difficulty, unresolved grief is dangerous. Freud said he looked upon "interference with mourning as harmful." The immediate short-range effects of unresolved grief may be to prolong mourning or to cause suffering beyond that demanded. There may even be physical or psychological difficulties that are not evident until much later. A London psychiatrist reported that 9 percent of his patients examined within a period of three years suffered from psychological problems set off by an experience of grief. Those who cannot eventually free themselves from their grief to build a new life should consult a doctor, minister, or social worker;

and psychiatry, that friend of mankind, may be suggested if that seems necessary.

This discussion may be considered an oversimplification by psychiatrists. They may add, "There is no normal." Perhaps "within the range of normality" would be a more precise way to put it. "This point is generally true but. . . ." The principles discussed *are* simplified, but let those of us who grieve have them as a start. We can go to psychiatrists if we get stuck on a "but."

These principles are presented in an approximate time order. They carry through from the first sharp, paralyzing experience of grief to the later period of eventual healing. Consequently, they apply to people in various phases. But as anyone knows who has gone through a serious personal loss, there are no clear lines between areas of experience. They merge and overlap each other. This information charts the vast area of unfamiliar emotions which those who grieve must face. Although this book speaks directly to the bereaved, it can give valuable insight to all who come in contact with people suffering grief—counselors, ministers, family, and friends.

2

The First Phase of Mourning

GRIEF IS AMONG THE DEEPEST PAINS that can be experienced and is a supreme test of a personality's ability to right itself. You who grieve may wonder how any written word can possibly help. What it can do is give you the benefit of what is known about grief, the accumulated wisdom of research. This shows what is happening to emotions during the inevitable mourning that follows death, and it also shows how to avoid destructive ways of handling those emotions. The printed word can give direction to help you do what only you can do—and that is resolve your grief. The resources for resolution *are* within you, even though you may not believe that possible.

When your life has been ripped to pieces by the death of someone central to it, you should not be surprised or ashamed of your reactions. Grief is met in many ways, from dazed calm to hysteria. People expect someone who has suffered lacerating physical damage to be incapacitated by pain. He is not able to react to anything except his intense, immediate suffering. Lacerating emotional damage can have the same effect. Realizing that you are in a state of emotional shock, you should not wonder at your sense of disbelief or your inability to accept your loss. It is normal for you to react to this overwhelming experience in ways that may seem abnormal to you. Other people have felt as you do.

Authorities believe that people consciously or unconsciously deny the death of those who have just died. An individual cannot separate himself immediately from the person who has died. A child separated from his mother may protest in angry howls demanding her return. Someone in grief often has the same response. He shows this response in *anger* at the frustration of separation and in *crying* as an appeal for help. He may even lash out at those he appeals to because they are unable to give him the help he demands.

Instead of denying the loss, others unconsciously and temporarily avoid it. One usually realistic woman got a telephone call which brought word of her college son's death in an automobile accident. She was in the house alone at the time and sat by the phone—not thinking or feeling—she just sat there. When she realized what had happened, she made a long distance call to her sister. This later proved to be a half hour after the first call, a half hour in which she had unconsciously protected herself from admitting her son's death.

An older woman who had nursed her husband through a long and painful illness started to get out of the car to go back to him as she was driven out of the cemetery after the funeral. She had taken care of him for so long that for a moment she felt that he still must need her. Then she fell back on the seat—not crying, staring ahead.

The head of a big office, a very efficient woman, lost a son in Vietnam. She had been widowed when he was still a baby and he had become the focal point of her life. When the son was killed, she could not believe it. "Nothing was real," she said, "and most of all, I couldn't accept that this was happening to me. The rest of the world went along as usual. People mowed their lawns and the milkman delivered the milk. But I was in a dream, a dreadful dream."

This first phase of mourning gradually disappears and you enter the second one—facing the reality of the death. This important second phase covers a long adjustment period when you need both guidance for yourself and recognition from others that you are experiencing a traumatic change in life.

The second phase of mourning eventually will get you through to the third and last phase, when your emotions finally begin to free themselves from mourning so that they can be invested in other interests. This gradually happens if you have permitted yourself—no, if you have forced yourself—to experience fully the healthy catharsis of painful mourning.

3

The Second Phase of Mourning

THE SECOND PHASE OF MOURNING is the crucial one, but there is little general understanding of what goes on during this time. Society understands no more about what you are going through than you do, and together, you and the people who surround you, operate in a psychological vacuum.

It is agreed by psychiatrists who write about grief that each person must go through the important "work of mourning." What this work requires can be quickly and simply stated, but it cannot be quickly and simply accomplished. The work of mourning requires that you, the bereaved, weaken and finally break every emotional tie to the past and every expectation for the future binding you to the person you have lost. Only by doing this can you ever be free emotionally to build a new life for yourself. Some authorities say that breaking the ties is so painful it is amazing that anyone can endure the hurt it requires, and they also say it is amazing that this pain in the lives of those who grieve is taken so for granted by others. This work takes weeks, months, and perhaps longer. No matter how reluctantly it is experienced, *it must be done.*

The image of Gulliver tied to the ground by the stakes and ropes of the Lilliputians represents the thousands of ties which bind you to the person you have lost. You and only you can break them, and then you and only you can form new ones—for there must be new ones if you are ever to be involved with life again—a new life, a different kind of life, one you believe (at the time) you can never accept.

During the first part of this phase, all your emotional energy is being invested in grief, and you can pay attention to nothing else.

A leading banker in a small farming community who was always known as a capable, self-reliant man was completely disorganized when his wife died suddenly of a heart attack. "I didn't know what to do," he said. "I mean I didn't know at all what to do. I sort of walked around, but why? I felt I must do something but couldn't. It wasn't at all like me. I wondered if I was going crazy. I couldn't even think what I would do without Ruth."

Such disorganization is natural and to be expected. Because this man could think of nothing but his wife and what her death meant to him, frustration thwarted him at every moment, and he found that the focus for his whole life was suddenly gone. Everything had a sense of unreality.

People even experience physical reactions in grief. A high school teacher made her home with her only relative, her sister.

When the sister died, the teacher experienced a sick, sinking feeling. "A little like the way you feel just after a near-accident—only it lasted longer. Besides that, I was almost too weak to walk across the room. . . . Everything I tried to do was such a terrible effort right after she died."

One woman who lost her husband had to use a wheel chair for a short time after his death, and she also felt choked and short of breath.

A retired man, whose wife of a lifetime died, said, "I didn't want to eat at all, and when I forced myself to, nothing had any taste."

The disorientations of grief seem so unfamiliar that people are often tempted to keep up a front or to take sedatives—anything to avoid an abandonment to it. But facing the loss and accepting the reality of it provide the best therapy possible.

Fear of insanity is sometimes a part of grief. Reactions are so unlike the usual self that insanity seems to be the only reasonable explanation. But those who grieve need not fear losing their minds in addition to suffering grief. The sharp pain of grief is a normal reaction to such a traumatic life change.

Every response to first grief need not be mentioned. But these people's reactions are typical, and will persist in varying degrees of severity for some time. Security, in many forms has vanished suddenly from your life, and as you cope with this all-absorbing inner experience, you have no energy left for anything else.

This experience is somewhat equivalent to the spontaneous collapse of a lung. You find you are operating on the oxygen that one lung can supply. You can't walk, you can't talk, you can't even move, for you have no energy. And if you do not know what has happened to you, you are terribly frightened. Through death you have a personal injury as great as this physical one, for you have been left without both real and intangible supports which have been part of the fabric of your whole life. Your experience can be just as keen, just as frightening, as the result of the sudden loss of oxygen.

There are no patterns to follow on what you should do during these first days. It does help to have people in your home who can answer the telephone and doorbell, because there will certainly be times when you are not able to. If seeing people who come to call will give you comfort, see them. If you want to stay by yourself or with a relative or close friend, do that. Others can meet friends who call. Be governed by what helps you and seems most natural to you.

After the funeral, the emergency atmosphere is over, usually the out-of-town family members have left, and the household begins whatever new life it is to assume.

Then the flowers fade and the dishes are returned—dishes that brought food for the bereaved, that strange, new person you have become; callers are less frequent. And you are faced with days, weeks, months of a new life. Now your task is to weaken and finally break the emotional ties that bind you to the person who has died. This is accomplished in several ways: first, by the private remembering that you experience constantly—by the welcome yet hurtful reminders that pour into your mind throughout every day and every night; second, by talking, by sharing your feelings and your thoughts with people who will listen endlessly and sympathetically; and third, less frequently, by writing. The thinking, the talking, and the writing need to go on freely as long as you require them.

Finally, a remarkable thing begins to happen. You notice that for short periods the hurt is not so great. This is the beginning of your healing. It means that *mentally* you have experienced your loss—over and over and over—and you are now moving into a time when you can accept it *emotionally.* This does not mean that you forget, but that you can remember without the emotions of grief tearing you apart as they did earlier. Almost without your realizing it, your emotions are being freed to become involved in other interests and activities.

This is a short summary of what *must* go on in the second phase. It is useful only as a framework into which to fit all that there is to say about this important time. Without such a framework, discussion of this period would seem fragmented.

The period of healing is long, and its changes should be gradual, so don't return to a life outside yourself too soon or too abruptly. What is too soon? Remembering the important work of mourning as the central necessity, follow your own needs. Don't be guided by what others think you should do. Do whatever gives you the greatest help.

Perhaps you want to be home alone in the comfort and pain of familiar surroundings. In this early grief you may want to have someone with you who is near whenever you need to talk—someone who understands and expects you will cry—someone for whom you need not censor your feelings. Authorities believe that having a loving person with you to share your grief helps more than anything else to resolve the inner conflicts you suffer and reduce the distress you feel. Family members quite naturally fill this important role. But an older woman I know whose husband died had no close family. However, she felt this need instinctively. When the funeral was over, she went to a town nearby to be with a friend who had also suffered from the loss, and they shared their sorrow.

As soon as you can do so without violating your important inner needs, slowly feel your way back to life outside yourself. You require outside experiences as soon as you have emotional energy free to invest in them. But if these experiences intrude too soon, they serve as surface distractions which interfere with the vital work of mourning. If you must make a constant effort, the outside is pushing in on you too soon. A friend whose daughter had been killed in an automobile accident came to have supper with me. We had planned that she come and leave as soon as she wanted to. But even in the short time she was with me, there were moments when she lost contact with the outside world and faded into herself. Still, it was good for her to come and try herself out in a quiet, short experience.

Neither seclusion nor the comfort of people who understand what you are going through can stretch into semi-permanent support. Although you feel you can never again be part of another life—one not connected with all you know you must wean yourself from—a beginning must be made. Don't make loneliness into a way of life. This would be a poor tribute to the person you have lost. Visit a friend. Try a business appointment or run some errands. Gradually lengthen the time you are with others when you must pay attention to something outside yourself. Increase the frequency of these experiences. There comes a time when you can gradually begin to change your focus from your inner needs to life outside yourself. You will sense when that time comes and will know how long and how often you can be comfortable allowing outside activity to come back into your life.

If you have work to return to, of course, you dread the first day back. It may help to decide if you want people to express sympathy and concern or whether you think you can manage better if you ask a friend to tell them not to say anything to you at first about your loss. If only a few people are involved, you probably will want to tell them yourself what would help you most. If possible, return to work for only part of a day for a while. Nothing but your own mourning will seem important to you and concentrating on other things for long periods displaces what should be going on in your mind. In fact, you cannot use your mind exclusively for anything else. It wanders, and it should. You will find that work is one of the biggest helps you have. Work forces you out of yourself; it gives your day focus and variety; it takes you away from home, the place you are probably reminded most deeply of your loss; it tires you so that you are glad to be home, and this helps you sleep better.

There is a warning. Don't pick up life outside yourself so soon that it interferes with your inner mourning.

Recovery from grief can be compared to recovery from a wound. A wound heals well if it gradually builds up healthy tissue —if the final scar covers such a good foundation that the healed wound does not prevent a person from leading a normal life. A wound that does *not* heal is one that has an infection preventing complete recovery. In grief the "infection" is made up of unresolved feelings that may come to life later, much later, in the form of emotional or physical problems. The body miraculously heals physical wounds. However, you can consciously take some part in healing the wound of your own grief.

Your attitude matters more than you realize. It can affect your health and wellbeing. According to Dr. Viktor Frankl, president of the Austrian Medical Society for Psycho-therapy: "Those who know how close the connection is between the state of mind of a man—his courage and hope or lack of them—and the state of immunity of his body will understand that the sudden loss of hope and courage can have a deadly effect." In discussing a man in a concentration camp, he says that the man's faith in the future and his will to live became paralyzed as the liberation date he dreamed of proved wrong. His body fell victim to illness and finally death.

As a person who is grieving, you are very different from your usual self because you *need* to be absorbed in the work of mourning. Often it is hard to be aware of or react to the world outside yourself.

Activities connected with the person you have lost are usually very absorbing. Writing notes of gratitude for kindness shown —even though painful to write—prolongs the old relationship through a necessary activity. A woman whose famous husband had just died threw herself into writing his biography. Some people get satisfaction from settling an estate or making out an income tax, projects that can legitimately prolong the association.

You are going through a completely frustrating experience. You turn to speak to someone—someone who will never again respond—"How was the baseball game?" or "I noticed that house we liked is almost finished," or "I made the sale!," or "A note came saying the yarn for your sweater is in," or "Now is the time for your medicine." You also find that many routine tasks had meaning only because they were associated with the person who died. And you meet frustration again. You may find it hard to make plans and carry them out, for you have nothing now you really want to do. Man can only live by looking to the future, and temporarily you have no future. Even your major work may lose its importance because it was done for a husband, a wife, a child, a parent, a sister, or a friend. Life now has no puurpose, as the whole structure of your inner dynamic has changed.

The thousands of associations and understandings you have built with the person you have lost now find no response. The jokes and expressions that no one else would think funny. The plans, the problems, and the fun you shared. One woman says she can never again linger over a second cup of morning coffee, the time of day when she and her husband talked together after the children went to school. Music or even certain tastes are reminders. There is no eye to catch in special understanding. For one man, packing for a trip became especially trying, since his wife had always done this for him. For married people "our" and "we" are words that can no longer be used. Then there wasn't enough time. Now there is too much. The changes are endless and entirely personal. Your despair, cruel as it is, is a sign that your grief is following the right pattern. It means you have accepted the death and are trying to adjust to what it means in your life.

Your life has broken into pieces—a bit of yourself a doctor's patient, another bit an employee, another a bowling team member, another a neighbor to drink coffee or beer with, and still another a friend to go to the movies with. You are used to being a total person, needed by someone else, always expected by someone else. You say you are going home. But where is home? One man whose wife had just died said he went home, yes, but nobody knew or cared. And what can you do on a vacation or a weekend?

A minister, representative of many counselors, asks all who come to him in grief to make a list of the ways in which everyday life has been changed because of the loss. Although it is hard to do, it begins a catharsis which forces you to think and feel each hurt that must be experienced. Breaking the generalized hurt down into the smallest parts help you weaken the ties to each one of the memories and expectations. Suffering is not so great if you can form a specific picture of it. Reading personal experience articles and books by people in grief may help. They record the stories of other people who have suffered, and yet survived somehow. In *The Rise of Silas Lapham,* William Dean Howells shows the universality of suffering when he says, "Many burdened souls . . . bowed down with the only misery like theirs in the universe; for each one of us must suffer long to himself before he can learn that he is but one in a great community of wretchedness which has been pitilessly repeating itself from the foundations of the world."

Catherine Marshall's book *To Live Again* has probably been more generally read by bereaved women than any other. Men can find help in C. S. Lewis's *A Grief Observed,* in which he describes his suffering when his wife died, and in John Gunther's *Death Be Not Proud,* an account of the courage this family displayed during the slow dying of the teen-age son.

You are not yourself in many ways. Your frustrations often make you react to other people with anger and hostility. I remember being disagreeable to a porter, and at the time realizing it was because I was covering up an anger that smoldered within me continually. I was angry at what had happened to me. I felt as though I were in severe pain and could not find a comfortable position in which to lie.

Being unusually sensitive and easily hurt may be another attitude you struggle with and yet try to cover. If you are uncomfortable keeping your emotions under control, don't go out in large groups. For a time confine yourself to small groups of close friends who will understand if you are suddenly short-tempered. Acting as you believe you should, instead of the way you feel, also makes you seem stiff and formal and unnatural. A relaxed and unusually outgoing teacher who had just lost her mother made a great effort to act like herself. Then a new student asked why she didn't like him. He wanted to know what he had done. Her honest answer choked her up a little, but the student caught a picture of a human being and lost the stereotype of a teacher.

The absorption in your inner task of

thinking and feeling through every new adjustment changes you. You may continue to be tired—so tired that you are enveloped in lethargy. As in any situation, it is easy to do something you want to do—and so difficult to do whatever you don't want to do, and now there's nothing you care about. C. S. Lewis said that he hadn't been aware before of the "laziness" of grief. You may go through your days with a frantic, compulsive sort of behavior, lunging at every task in a flurry of determination—again an outward effort to battle the inward pull of concentration on the work of mourning. You may withdraw from any activity, a very natural way to adjust to your demanding inner needs, but you must eventually find your way back to a life outside of yourself; or you may go through a restless, ineffectual flitting from one thing to another—hardly aware of what you are doing, so absorbing is your inner turmoil.

A chief dilemma of those who grieve is their reluctance to break the ties with the person who has died. Acceptance of the reality of death means never avoiding a chance to think of the loss and all its ramifications. Getting used to it, familiar with it, learning to live with it—these lead to full acceptance. However, you may be constantly torn between the need to suffer deeply and the almost overpowering inclination to escape suffering through any surface diversions or through drink or drugs. Camus has caught the essence of this problem in *The Plague:* "They forced themselves never to think, to cease looking to the future, and always to keep, so to speak, their eyes fixed on the ground at their feet. But, naturally enough, this prudence, this habit of feinting with their predicament and refusing to put up a fight, was ill rewarded. For, while averting that which they found so unbearable, they also deprived themselves of redeeming moments, frequent enough when all is told. Thus, in a middle course between heights and depths, they drifted through life rather than lived, the prey of aimless days and sterile memories, like wandering shadows that could have acquired substance only by consenting to root themselves in the solid earth of their distress."

Facing reality is the only path to take in seeking the road to recovery. Marcel Proust said, "We are healed of a suffering only by experiencing it to the full." Postponing the work of mourning only makes it more difficult. Experiencing the hurt is necessary, for it helps us face the present by reducing the hold of the past—the past which included associations that can never again be a part of the present or the future.

At the same time that you are absorbed by your grief you may be experiencing some unexpected emotions. One of them is guilt. Sometimes this guilt centers around a last illness. A mother told me that she had asked herself a thousand times if she should have insisted on having another doctor as consultant during her teenage daughter's long illness with cancer.

A sister felt she could never get over her guilt at not keeping the night nurse. She said, "My sister died alone—in the night.

almost unbearable frustrations with which you are already burdened. Physical exertion can help to dispel this unwanted energy. An interior decorator whose two sons were serving on active duty in World War II got a job rather than stay home, and so her fear and nervous energy were partially dissipated. In *Mama's Bank Account* the immigrant mother, worried about her daughter in the hospital, rewashed the newly scrubbed kitchen floor.

Physical exercise helps temporarily, but relating to life again, seeing some plan take shape for your future, gradually dispels fear permanently. Fear, although bewildering, is not so threatening if the causes and ways of meeting it are understood.

You who are in severe grief know the feeling that you do not want to live. Why should you want to? What will you live for? An ex-service man told me that when his son was drowned in a diving accident, his first thought was to kill himself. To prevent his doing this in an irrational moment, he emptied his service revolver of its shells and threw them away so that his suicide would have to be deliberate. Some part of him did not truly want death.

I had an experience that illustrates this same important but little recognized factor. It happened a few months after my husband died. I was driving with the windows closed and could hear only the whir of the motor. I turned a corner onto a railroad track and saw a train—racing at me just yards away. Strangely calm, I jammed down the accelerator, the car lurched ahead, and the train thundered past my rear window. Trembling, I pulled to the side of the road. Then suddenly I realized I had only one conscious thought—a bitter regret that I had not been killed. Yet something had compelled me to speed up to escape death. Did I unknowingly want to live? Was I telling myself that I could accept life without him? Something had made me deny death and gravitate toward life. Like the ex-service man, I did not truly want death.

This unconscious pull toward life is an unrecognized ally helping people who grieve. A person has a limitless capacity to move forward. Carl Rogers, the psychologist, calls this "the main spring of life." It helps people reach out toward life as surely as plants grow toward light. This pull toward life not only operates to prevent suicide, but also unconsciously motivates people to rebuild life.

Those who grieve are not the only ones who seek a rebirth. The divorced and those suffering a major physical disability such as blindness, disfigurement, or crippling are among those who are motivated by this same vital pull. They, too, must gradually break the ties to their old lives and build new ones. They must finally accept and adjust to a new way of life—one they do not want—but one open to them. One remarkable person who has created a life in spite of two crippling experiences, the death of her husband and blindness, called this rebuilding of life a big do-it-yourself job. And it is exactly that.

There are many ways of bringing about this eventual new life and of achieving acceptance of it. They involve an elaboration of the talking, writing, and thinking process mentioned earlier.

Talking out experiences and feelings is a natural way to learn to accept them. Friends who want to help may offer the gift of themselves as available and truly sympathetic listeners. However, you will find that some friends can do this for you and some cannot. I know a woman who did not want to involve friends. She paid a psychologist five dollars an hour to listen as she talked through every emotion of her grief over her son's death. She realized she needed to make herself familiar with and accept the hard things she had to say.

Some time after her brother's death, an older woman told me how grateful she was to a cousin who came to spend a week with her. "Now say anything you need to to me. Don't try to say what you think you should. Be honest. You may not always say complimentary things about George. That's all right. He can't become suddenly perfect just because he died. You'll feel better if you talk and talk and talk."

There are times when you need to talk endlessly about your loss. This helps relive the experiences you long to return to, and the very talking about the past makes you accept the fact that such experiences can never take place again. In other words, this talking helps you to face reality—the only basis on which an adjustment can be made to any problem. You need to talk about the seemingly barren future, the bits of encouragement that dissolve, and the practical decisions that have to be made.

Also there is writing as a catharsis—a method seldom used. Some people, in addition to making the list suggested by the minister, keep a journal. A friend who lost a sister told me that she kept a journal, a day-in-and-day-out account of every experience, every thought, every feeling. Some people may think this is morbid. Others will recognize it as good therapy, for one who grieves cannot afford to repress anything. C. S. Lewis relates in *A Grief Observed* that he began writing in notebooks that he found around the house—filling them by recounting every aspect of his despair, loneliness, and anger.

One woman told me that she wrote to her mother who had died—wrote to her about her yearnings and fears, even of her guilt over things she had not done for her. She kept this journal for months as a way to learn to accept the feelings she wanted to bring into the open and learn to live with. Writing this book has helped me express accurately how I feel. Writing must have helped C. S. Lewis, Catherine Marshall, and all the others who have written about their experiences with grief.

Last, there is thinking. No inner or outer censor, however strict, can keep you who grieve from thinking almost continously of the one you have lost. Someone has said that the best remedy for any misery is to think that misery through to the end. This you do constantly.

An experience of mine illustrates so many facets of this period that it is worth telling just as it happened. Some time after my husband's death, I was marketing, a task I had come to hate because I had no one to market for but myself—no one else's tastes to consider. At the vegetable counter I reached for some fresh asparagus. How my husband loved it. But no. I wouldn't take any. The bunches were too big for one person and why bother to fix it just for myself? I trudged on. "La Traviata" poured in from the loud speaker. It followed me all the way to the meat counter. Then that lovely, long note, a moment when he always caught my eye! There were some fillets on the counter. The first time I cleaned the freezer, I had found two fillets —just two. We had bought them together on just such an afternoon's marketing trip, bought them as a special treat. But we'd never had them, and there they were, every time I went to the freezer.

Macademia nuts. How he fussed when I

got them for him. I could hear his standard protest, "But eighty cents is just too much for forty-three superb nuts."

The supermarket carries playing cards. The hours we spent at canasta! By this time I was near tears. Then I saw a teacher, one I wanted to avoid, so I slipped around a counter only to run into her at the next corner. She immediately began to complain about her problem students, long-ago research difficulties in biology, and her dreary and self-centered plans for the summer. I sidled along the aisles as she followed me in spite of my saying I must get home. Finally, escaping to the check-out stand, I waited my turn. As I stood there, I suddenly saw how little she had. Only books and bugs and herself. For the first time I could honestly feel grateful for what life had given me. Just then a close friend came into the store. I knew her husband was out of town, so I asked her for dinner. "Let's see, I could have those two fillets and some biscuits with the red raspberry jam I made and hoarded for my husband and—

oh, yes—some asparagus." And I was off to grab some and hurry home.

This illustrates so much more than the constant reminding. There is the insight that changed my feelings. This change of *feeling* is a most important change to achieve. I changed from being sorry for myself to honestly feeling grateful. Then there is the invitation to dinner—a spontaneous act that carried me out of myself—an example of the kind of thing representative of the third phase, when it is possible to invest some emotional interest in something outside yourself. For a short period I was not simply going through the motions of living. And with this came a change in the attitude toward the fillets, the jam, and the asparagus. They were important for their own sakes; they were no longer preserved as memorials to my husband.

Of course, no experience can be relived. But I doubt that I would have extended that invitation to dinner had I met my friend when I was absorbed in self-pity. I don't know. This one experience did not in itself mark a complete turning point, but it was a beginning. It shows the feelings and attitudes that flow between the second and third phases of mourning. Finally, there is an inner change—it could be called growth —that must take place in spite of each person's resistance to it.

Incidents like this—many of them—experienced over and over in the months of mourning, gradually help you invest less of your emotional energy in remembering the person you have lost, and thus more can be used for something else. But how can this happen? That's not as important as the living proof you see every day that it does happen. President Eisenhower in the films shown for his memorial said that he had never gotten over the death of his three-year-old son. He thought of all the little boy could have been and done. But the death of President Eisenhower's son certainly did not keep him from living a full life. He got over it emotionally, though he remembered it intellectually.

Some people who are bogged down in

grief would almost welcome some disaster, so great is their need to be blasted out of themselves. A friend's personal disaster helped a grieving college boy I knew. He was deeply in love and engaged. He was to be married in three months and he checked off the days—one by one. Sixty—fifty—forty, and finally the count was down to twenty-three. Then his fiancée was murdered in her apartment. It was never discovered who did it or why. A senseless, unsolved crime. Suddenly she was gone. There was no clue.

John found it almost impossible to concentrate on his work. He went through the experiences of mourning—all of them. He tried his old distractions, beer and parties. But here the chatter seemed rattling and shallow: silly people saying words. What had once been fun was now an intrusion on his important inner experience. He wanted to get beyond himself and his hurt, but he couldn't. He needed something compelling enough to jolt him out of himself.

Then he found a break-through. Dave,

an alcoholic friend, needed help. John found him sick with drink one Saturday night in a dormitory and called the infirmary. It was against their rules to dry out alcoholics; perhaps a private hospital would take his friend. But there was no money for a private hospital. Finally, John talked to Dave's doctor, and he prescribed a method of treatment. Dave should be given a heavy dose of a tranquilizer every four hours and kept from drinking. This was the important thing—because the tranquilizers and drink must not be taken together. The results, as in the death of a famous television star, could be fatal. The doctor told John to call him at home if there was real trouble. John possessed some of these tranquilizers, for he had tried that route to ease his own pain. So he took over Dave and his problem.

His first step was to get him to his own apartment, help him undress, and give him the first dose of tranquilizers. He was going to put him to bed, but Dave passed out on the couch in the living room before he got that far. John locked the little liquor he had and Dave's clothes in his bedroom closet.

As the tranquilizers wore off, the struggle began. Dave wanted a drink, a very little one to get him through—only one. When he couldn't persuade John to give him that, he got up to go to the bathroom and casually stopped by the liquor closet on the way back to the couch. Nothing there? He threw himself down on the couch. There was only an hour and a half to go. The two began to talk—mostly about Dave's war experiences—the men's eyes as he knifed their bellies and twisted the knife to be sure they were done for.

But the need for a drink kept coming up. Dave was restless. Wouldn't John drive him to his room? He had some liquor in his closet. It wouldn't take long. If John wouldn't, he'd walk there. Then he found his clothes were gone. He was more than restless. He was panicky. John wondered if perhaps this wasn't the time to call the doctor. But it was two in the morning, and he hated to wake him. There were only forty-five minutes left. Maybe they could make it to the next dose.

Then Dave grabbed the phone and began to dial. He had a friend who would bring him liquor. Somebody he just called and who always came—for a sum. There was a fight for the telephone. In the struggle, the cord tore out of the wall. Dave lay on the floor and whimpered. The physical effort of the fight had helped him, though. He was calmer.

Now Dave was in a corner. No liquor, no clothes, no telephone. He said that a hot bath sometimes helped him—relaxed him. So John filled the tub. As Dave lay in the steaming water, the two talked, mostly of how Dave got hooked. They talked and watched the clock together. Dave held on to John's hand now—grasped it as something solid he could trust to help him through. For John had proved he was solid. He had outfoxed Dave in all the tricks he had played. Together they watched as the second hand ticked around the clock. The moment came. Dave could have his second dose.

For an hour or so after this dose Dave slept. John began to doze in a chair beside him when he suddenly woke. He realized that all that night he hadn't thought of his own troubles. He had concentrated so on his effort to help Dave by keeping him talking and by outthinking him that his mind and emotions had been completely engaged. For the first time since his fiancee's death he had been able to forget himself. He had been truly blasted out of himself by Dave's emergency. This happened at a time when he was emotionally ready—but he himself had had to sense this and so open himself up to such an involvement.

One obstacle that frequently prevents the full acceptance of grief is a failure to recognize the need, the absolute necessity, of releasing damaging emotions by crying. Of course, there are times—many, many of them—when there is nothing else you can do. But as time passes you may try to control your emotions, to make yourself behave as you believe a disciplined person should. When you are on the verge of tears, you must concentrate on keeping control. This makes it difficult to reach out to experiences that could become important new involvements or interests. Children in school react sometimes in the same way. They fear not getting right answers or good grades, and the fear consumes so much thought and feeling that there is little left for the real challenge of learning. You will find that "a good cry," that seemingly contradictory term, sets you free so that you can become involved eventually in something outside yourself. A wise old man once said, "Cry it out. All that grief inside makes you sick, like poison." The recovery from grief comes from experiencing it as *acutely* as possible. You'll find after a complete catharsis that you feel better. Tears are meant to release tension. Use them for that purpose.

If you can, give in to such grief in private

so that you won't unexpectedly overflow in public where other people, often strangers, get involved. A kind word, an unexpected reminder, someone in a crowd who by the tilt of the head or a way of walking reminds you of the person you have lost—these are the things that catch you unawares. Then there are the times when your mind is not busy. This leaves it empty to dwell on what might have been, on what you have lost. Standing in line in a supermarket or a movie, walking or driving, sitting on a bus or a train, are times when it is easy for unexpressed emotions to overflow. Awareness of information such as this cannot by itself suddenly free you from grief, but it can give you an understanding of how to handle your emotions. You will be sorrowing yet not be out of control.

And so the long hard task of the second phase of mourning must go on until your emotions begin to work themselves out. Time helps, but time alone is not enough. During the passing of time you must know that you are working in the right direction.

You must not unknowingly defeat your ultimate purpose of finding a way back to a life that you can live.

4

Society's Influence

WHILE YOU ARE ATTEMPTING TO ADJUST to grief, you are not living in a social vacuum. You are in a society that has an important influence on you. Surprising as it may seem, there are factors in this society that make a sound adjustment to grief especially difficult although *you* may be working in the right direction.

If you have not been aware of society's attitude, a few quotations will illustrate the difficulties. Elton McNeil, a psychologist from the University of Michigan, says in his book, *Human Socialization,* "Our culture has sanitized and denied death as a fact of life." This reflects a cogent comment of Margaret Mead, the anthropologist. "We celebrate birth and a wedding and then pretend there is no death." A minister on a David Susskind television program said, "The whole culture denies death." George W. Cornell, an Associated Press religious writer, declares, "Modern culture tries to obscure death and avoid talk of it." A thorough study of society's attitude toward death was made by Geoffrey Gorer, a British anthropologist. He says that his evidence suggests that his findings hold true for both the United States and Britain. The main theme of his book, *Death, Grief, and Mourning,* is that there is a "social denial and individual repudiation of mourning." He believes that a reason for this may be the increasing pressure of the "fun-morality." "The majority of both countries tends to treat mourning as morbid self-indulgence, and to give social admiration to the bereaved who hide their grief so fully that none would guess anything had happened."

This general avoidance of the recognition of death makes it difficult for you, a person grieving in the midst of such a society, to carry on a thorough process of mourning. You perhaps have recognized instinctively what helps you most in working through your grief, but faced with the daily reality of society's attitude toward grief, you may not be able to follow your own common sense. You may have adopted society's attitude and attempted "the individual repudiation of mourning" unknowingly.

Society's attitude actually discourages vital grief work. According to the British study, the bereaved are not given the support they need. "Mourning is treated as if it were a weakness . . . an irresponsible bad habit instead of a psychological necessity." Society is certainly not actively cruel or indifferent. People simply do not realize what is required of a person who is grieving. Furthermore, when most of the information known about grief can be found only in professional literature, it is understandable that most members of society are unaware of what they should expect and how they should react during the period of distress caused by a death.

Another aspect of society's influence on those who grieve is evidenced in the disappearance of the year-long mourning rituals. According to the British survey, this trend is true of "English speaking countries with a Protestant tradition." We would not have the rituals revived: the crepe on the door and the drawn blinds which marked a house of mourning for all who passed by; people speaking softly and walking in dignity, paying respect, even anonymous respect, to the symbols of death. Mourners were recognized as people suffering from a special problem in their year of mourning identified by black armbands for the men and black mourning clothes for the women. All this symbolism would seem inappropriate in today's society, but as Willy Loman's wife says in *Death of a Salesman,* "Attention should be paid." People do not realize "the mighty effort" that must be made when tragedy comes. From what they have seen going on around them, they believe there is nothing to going through such an adjustment.

Anthropologists report that the mourning rituals of primitive tribes, the wakes of some countries, and the period of ritualized mourning by Jews serve special purposes during bereavement. I wrote Rabbi Eugene Lipman of Temple Sinai in Washington, D.C., to ask about the Jewish rituals of mourning. His answer shows the remarkable insight which the fathers of Judaism used in developing the rituals following death. They recognized the need to mourn, the need to give community support to mourning, the need to take specific time for mourning.

> Jewish law worked out response to death in a sequence which is, I think, totally consistent with what I know of people and their real needs.
>
> 1. From the time of death until the funeral the survivors are left to themselves. All external matters are taken

care of for them by others—food is provided, the house is taken care of, business is closed. One does not comfort them yet—they are considered to be in shock and should be left to their grief.

2. The funeral is important. Psalms are read—they say what we want to say and can't, and they have a special magic anyhow. A eulogy is mandatory, with rare exceptions. There is a mourner's prayer. At the cemetery, the ritual is brief. After burial—which is completed while everyone is present, and usually with everyone participating—family and friends form parallel lines facing in, and the mourners walk between the lines and people say the formula: "May God comfort you together with all the mourners of Zion and Jerusalem."

3. "Shiva" is observed. The word means "seven," but it rarely involves seven full days. During Shiva, the family remains at home, and friends

come to visit. Ideally, they all sit together and talk. In practice, there is lots of food and, by the end of the week, some gaiety. Without exception, every mourning family I have known has derived enormous comfort from the Shiva days and evenings.

4. "Shloshim" is observed. This means "thirty," and it lasts for a month after the death. Then the men go back to work, the children go back to school, the women go about their various occupations. There are no social gatherings or parties, but all routines are carried on during this period.

5. For eleven months after the death, designated people (close relatives) go to the synagogue a stated number of times a week and during the service say the Kaddish, the mourner's prayer.

6. Each year after that, in perpetuity, on the anniversary of the

death, the designated people go to the synagogue and recite the Kaddish during services.

7. On stated occasions during the year there is a Yizkor, a memorial service for all deceased, and the Kaddish is said by all the designated people.

I'm fascinated by the fidelity of response among Jews who knew none of the customs from childhood or training but who responded at the time of mourning. It seems clear that my forefathers gauged their people well.

Today there are still rituals for the first few days of mourning—from the time of the death to the funeral. We send flowers and food, cards and letters; we donate money to special funds and books to libraries. Close friends call and offer to help by doing errands, furnishing guest rooms, taking care of children or old people who are part of the mourning household, answering the door and telephone, going to meet relatives from out of town. Then, of course, friends and associates attend the funeral.

All these kindnesses are gratefully accepted. We have all heard bereaved people say that they didn't believe they could have gotten through the first days without the feeling of support that surrounded them. But there are no further rituals through which to express concern. After the funeral some people call; more flowers are sent; cards and letters arrive for a while. A few people continue to be truly helpful and understanding. But the general attitude, either implied or actually spoken, is, "Think about something else. That's the best way," a poor approach were it possible to follow it. For it is harmful psychologically to interrupt the helpful work of mourning.

Also, people are not comfortable with you if you are mourning. According to Dr. David Peretz, of Columbia University, "The dominant social expectation of one bereaved is that he will quickly pick up his pattern of life . . . and be quiet about his grief. With this ethos, the lack of support from family, friends and neighbors will force the bereaved to abandon his grief prematurely." C. S. Lewis confessed he felt he was "an embarrassment to people." Friends seem to want you back to normal as soon as possible so they can then be at ease with you once more. You, the one grieving, are expected to adjust to society's requirements.

In an attempt to find acceptance, according to anthropological studies, some people today repudiate mourning. If there is private denial of grief, the ties to the deceased are not broken as they should be in the slow, thorough process of mourning; rather the ties are buried. In addition, the comfort of crying is suppressed, and the release of damaging emotions is not as complete or frequent as it should be. Grieving friends apologize for crying, even in private conversations, and attempt to choke off tears. They reflect an attitude of present-day society that is a far cry from the wailing rituals common to other societies. Not that we should welcome wailing rituals, but we do need a healthier and more understanding approach to the needs of those who mourn.

One last aspect of society that makes death unreal is the manner in which we have depersonalized death. At one time death was a part of the everyday experience of the community. A dying person remained in his household. The family gathered, and community concern was concentrated on him. Melanie's death scene in *Gone With the Wind* depicts the close family love experienced at such a time. It was customary for the body to lie in state in the parlor for a day or two, and again death's reality was evident. Within the memory of many people today, death and funerals were part of home life. I remember six funerals that were held in my own family home.

Now death has been institutionalized. People die in hospitals or nursing homes, and services for them are held in other institutions, churches, or funeral parlors. Frequently, there is no coffin, either open or closed. The body has been cremated or donated to medical research. Although efficient, all this contributes to the lack of belief in death's reality.

In addition to the diminishing support which society affords people adjusting to a death, institutions which formerly provided the bereaved great comfort are now less useful than they used to be. One of these institutions is the church. True religious faith that has long sustained people through grief is not the help that it was in the past. Life has been impoverished by the diminishing influence of religion. Many people are not sustained by the strength that religion has to give. This resource, once so deep and widespread, is no longer as important to them, and it is not even a part of life to a great number.

The English anthropological study states "a minority of the bereaved are convinced adherents of religious creeds, . . . a majority . . . have neither religious help nor guidance in this crisis of loneliness."

The depersonalization of metropolitan living does not impose community influence on people to become a part of a religious institution. Those who do join churches are often a part of a large congregation, where it is difficult for ministers to know church members in a close, personal way. The predominant influence of science has, no doubt, also contributed to a lessening of religious faith.

Whatever the reasons for religion's reduced influence, it is important to realize that the minister is no longer the person to whom many people turn as a source of first comfort. And the service itself, although religious in nature, does not provide the solace that it once gave the bereaved who were adherents of a strong religious tradition. Consequently, the church does not give comfort to as many people who grieve as it formerly did.

The family is another institution that, in general, does not sustain people in grief as it has in the past. Of course family influence can vary widely. Some people have no family at all while others are enclosed in a network of loving relationships. However, the family is less of a resource in time of need than it was a generation ago when people were less mobile and families tended to remain in one community. Today family members frequently live in another part of this country or the world. There were also large houses in which a variety of generations lived—either happily or unhappily—but at least there was a place in which a single person could belong to a life larger than his own. Aunts, uncles, and grandparents were a part of households twenty-five years ago. Today's houses are smaller, and society has gradually put a single person into a solo role.

There is a trend, now often found by mutual consent, for each family member living in the same community to maintain separate living arrangements and a separate social life. Two sisters live in the same neighborhood, both are widowed, yet each has kept her own house. A mother and son in the same town live in separate apartments. A grown daughter has her own house although her parents live nearby in the old family home. The family does not usually make a way of life. It supplements it. In addition, many families today have been fragmented by divorce and remarriage. Contemporary families are often made up of step-parents, step-children, and half-brothers and sisters. Consequently, the likelihood of intimate family relationship is diminished.

Families that are remote either geographically or emotionally make it difficult for anyone who is trying to survive grief. This is especially true because, as previously stated, a chief source of comfort for the mourner is to be near people who love him and share his grief. Grief can be resolved more easily and more quickly if those closest to the person who has died experience their sorrow together.

It is true that formerly people knew no more about what they experienced in grief than they know today. People have rarely been aware of precisely what was psychologically useful in resolving grief. But institutions formerly were more useful in helping the individual cope with mourning. Society was more understanding of death. Mourning rituals gave those who grieved special recognition. The church supported them spiritually. And the family tended to be close so that shared mourning gave them all a natural opportunity for effective therapy.

Today every one of these institutions is less effective than formerly in its support of those in grief. Certain fortunate individuals may still be sustained by one or more of them. But generally this is not the case. Each person is left quite on his own in a society that understands no more of what he is experiencing than he does. Neither the individual nor the society recognizes the toll that mourning takes. And the lack of understanding encourages the poorest possible long-range therapy—superficial mourning and the suppression of damaging emotions.

But there is help for those who grieve. The simple psychology of normal grief can be understood, accepted, and put to use as generally as is the psychology of other specialized areas: psychology of childhood, of adolescence, of learning. Were society aware and acceptant of the work of grief, you who grieve would not be expected to "be yourself" any more than someone who has just had a major operation. It would be taken for granted that time and loving attention are needed to recover from both.

5

The Help of Friends

WITH THE UNDERSTANDING YOU NOW HAVE of the process of mourning, you will sense what friends should do to help and what they should not do. Close friends are second only to loving family members in their importance to someone in grief. Because the way your friends feel and act is vital in helping—or hindering—your work of mourning, this section, although addressed to you, is written for them.

There is much that a close friend can do. Chiefly, he can show you that he cares for you and is concerned about what you are going through. During the first days, at least one person should be in close touch with you to give you comfort and stability in the confusion of emotion and activity which surrounds you. It should be someone *you* want—not just anyone who may want to do this for you. Those in grief are sometimes subjected to the attention of people they do not welcome in this intimate role. The person near you need not be a family member if you feel you would rather be with a friend. You are the one who needs support, and what you want is all important. As you should do whatever you can for yourself, this person should supplement you when there is something you are not able to work out for yourself. You may need this kind of help temporarily.

Other close friends and neighbors will want to take over the management of your home by assuming responsibility for the telephone, callers, meals, errands—details you do not want to think about. This leaves you free as you should be at this time. Let these friends do whatever they offer because they want to have some part in helping you and they want to express their sympathy for you in action as well as words.

The sense of emergency and the necessary activities carry you through the first few days. Then follow the long days of the second phase of mourning, and it is during this time that friends can be of the greatest help. If family members do not live near, you will be completely dependent on friends and neighbors to sustain you. Sometimes you share with another a mutual grief. This is true of parents who mourn a child; brothers and sisters who mourn a parent; or friends who mourn a friend. But often you are left alone to find your way.

1. Your friends can help in many ways. During early grief a day is a little easier to get through if you know you can be with someone in the late afternoon and evening.

You may not want to be with others often, but you want to know you can be, if this helps you. Afternoon is the time of day when children come home from school, when people meet after a day's work, when someone came home to you or when you came home to someone. Dinners are remembered as times you shared, not times you ate a meal.

It would help if a friend called you ahead and gave you a choice of nights when you could come to dinner. Leaving the choice of the date up to you helps because you have the comfort of knowing a certain night is filled—and this is usually important to you. One woman whose little girl had been killed in an automobile accident was left alone when her husband had to go out of town. Her close friends got together and one of them asked her for dinner each night so that she was never alone in the evening unless she wanted to be.

2. The greatest help for you will be knowing people you can feel free to go to at any time when you desperately need com-

panionship and understanding. This point should be double-starred because it is so important, especially if you have been left alone in your grief. However, a "come any time" invitation must be preceded by many specific ones or you won't feel like following up on it.

3. Another important gift, one you truly need, is that of listening. It is one that your close friends usually give. You want friends who will listen meaningfully as you try to break the ties to the person you have lost, as you talk about your feelings—those strange, new feelings so hard to describe and understand—talking, talking as you try to come to terms with this experience you don't want to believe. Someone who stares ahead or who gets restless or who changes the subject is not listening meaningfully. You need a few people who care enough to hear you out again and again.

4. This is a time when you have little initiative, for you are using your energy in the work of mourning. C. S. Lewis calls this the "laziness of grief." Consequently, you

want friends to be sensitive to your needs. You may send out an indirect cry for help by telephoning or stopping by to visit. Perhaps you are ready for a little activity outside yourself. But you may not know where to begin and would be grateful to have a friend who is thoughtful enough to plan something for you to do once in a while. If you don't feel like doing what you are invited for, you certainly need not accept. But it is good to be remembered and asked. You need to feed activities into your life gradually as your emotions begin to free themselves from the past and as you are ready to pay attention to something beside your own work of mourning.

5. Many people will not want to speak of your loss for fear of hurting you. Yet often it helps you to listen to others speak of how much they loved or how much they miss the person who has died. You also welcome natural references to your old life. You don't want people to shy away from the past as though it had never been.

6. During this time your feelings may be

easily hurt, and friends can help if they go a little out of their way for you. I overheard a woman invite a recently widowed friend for dinner and offer to pick her up. "No. I must learn to drive by myself at night. I might as well begin now." However, it must have been a comfort to have the offer of this special attention.

Of course, the opposite of all these suggestions is exactly what friends should *not* do.

1. Friends should not invite you for dinner at the last moment unless they have had you many times since your bereavement. Nor should they invite you for a certain date without considering your convenience. If you cannot accept on that one date, they may feel their obligation to you has been fulfilled and not ask you again. But it is your needs, not their convenience, that should be considered. For this one invitation you are special.

2. If a friend tries to distract you and make you talk about something beside your problems before you are ready, he

shows no understanding of what you are going through in early grief. What he is saying indirectly is, "When you are like yourself again, I'll be more comfortable with you." People who are lonely in grief are tempted to act on such advice because they may be so in need of companionship that they try to fit in with what is expected of them. You do not want the whole society to help you carry your grief, but close friends should be able to do it for you. However, you may be surprised to learn that it is the quality of the person rather than the closeness of the relationship that prompts empathetic concern. Suggesting that someone forget his grief is the poorest possible advice to give right after a death. Yet it is just such advice as this, multipled many times over, that created a society that prompts people to repudiate private mourning. As you now know, unresolved grief and "repudiation of mourning" are dangerous, for they censor and slow up the breaking of the ties to the person lost. This may prolong unnecessarily the work of mourning and may also make it more painful than it need be; and it is already painful enough.

3. If people try to take over your life, they are acting out of a need to dominate rather than a desire to help. "Taking over" means domineering consistently rather than encouraging the signs of returning initiative within you. Those who fill in as they become alert to your needs are not dominating but are encouraging you in your first efforts to take a step toward interests outside yourself.

4. People should not do what is natural and meaningful for them rather than what is most helpful for you.

5. People should not urge sedatives on you. You need to work through your mourning, not postpone it. Your doctor would understand how important it is for you to be free to mourn, so be governed only by his advice.

6. People should not be casual about offering sympathy. A man who met me six weeks after my husband died called back

as he passed, "Oh, sorry about your husband," in as cheerful and offhand a way as though he had said, "Pretty day, isn't it?" This attitude is shown by the people who come to pay a sympathy call and then stay indefinitely to talk about their own affairs.

These two suggested lists of the applications of the psychology of grief and your own understanding of that psychology will help you evaluate what people say and do. You will know what will help or hinder you in your efforts to get through the painful work of mourning. You can see now the importance of the statement: "The way friends feel and act is vital in helping—or hindering—your work of mourning."

6

Practical Decisions

SIDE BY SIDE with your important inner needs, there are practical steps that should be taken during the second phase of mourning. You will have expert advice on various business and legal decisions. But it is just as important to make wise personal decisions, decisions that are in accord with what good psychology dictates.

A task that must eventually be undertaken is the disposal of the belongings of the person who has died. Much as it hurts, it is wise to do this early in the second phase of mourning. At this time some family member is probably still with you, and together you can decide on what to do with each of the articles which is no longer needed. Of course, there are special items that you yourself would like to have. Then certain pieces of clothing and jewelry you probably will want to give to members of the family or friends who would want to have them for their personal association as well as their utilitarian value. If you can, it might help you to make these gifts yourself. If you do not want to, the person working with you can see to it that they are given in your name.

All other belongings can be donated to

some organization which distributes them to people who can use them. These organizations usually pick up such gifts.

Personal belongings left untouched for long may become "shrines" difficult to disturb. We all know or have heard of people who display rooms that are kept "just as they were," visible ties to the person who died, ties that have not been broken over the years. The disposal of personal belongings intimately associated with the one you mourn is a hard task, a heartbreaking one, if you will. The longer it is put off, the more time, thought, and emotion you spend in dreading the task. Spare yourself this. Disposing of these belongings gives you a useful and necessary association with the past, and although this is a sad comfort, it is a comfort.

While it is best to dispose early of the personal belongings that must be given away, major decisions such as selling a house or moving to another community should be postponed, if possible, until you are more like yourself. It is better to live through the second phase of mourning in a home familiar to you. A home represents security that you need if keeping it is not a financial burden. Much else has changed in your life, but your home can remain solid. You may emotionally outgrow the need for it as your life takes on a different pattern. Then you can sell it, but having sold it and made the hundreds of decisions which you must when dismantling it, you can, of course, never have it back no matter how much you regret having let it go. A couple whose only son died decided in good time to adopt children, as many as they could afford. They wanted a home where there was a pasture for horses and a brook for fishing. They planned their new home entirely around the needs of children, and looking toward the future and not the past, they moved to a country place with anticipation and excitement. This was all done "in good time," not immediately after the death of their own little boy.

You may be tempted to go to another community to live near or with someone in your family who represents the emotional security which, very naturally, you long for. But wait. Moving to another community is obviously an even more far-reaching change than selling a home. If you want to move to a community where you have many friends and activities, you are on safer ground than if you are moving to one where your only tie is a single family. This is especially true if the family is younger than you are. You may enjoy their friends, but you will have little to base new friendship on because their interests cannot be your interests. And a younger family may have to move, leaving you a stranger in a strange community at a time when you need old friends.

An unusually attractive woman in her sixties moved to a new town to be near her married daughter. But she never felt at home there. Although she was interested in making new friends, most women her age were in a period of their lives when their contacts had been long established and their friendships had become static.

Of course, there may be situations when you can easily, if not gladly, give up a home or community that you have outgrown, but this is not usual.

Often, as time passes, decisions make themselves. You develop an emotional readiness that shows you clearly what should be done. I would have felt dispossessed had I sold my home soon after my husband's death. But much later, without making a conscious decision, I walked up to a real estate man at a meeting and put my house on the market. I had long realized that this was a practical step to take. I do not pretend to know what evolved within me that made this possible. I merely offer it as an example of what I mean by "emotional readiness."

Selling a home or going to live in another community may be good steps to take in the long run. The same decision may be a seasoned and wise one when made in the third phase of mourning, but if made prematurely during the second phase, you may look back on it with regret for a lifetime. Try staying in your home and community until you are sure that you no longer need them—until you find that your security is within yourself. Then you will be free to do whatever your new life demands.

Something which you may not have thought about is the importance of being in good physical condition as you go through the emotional strain of the second phase of mourning. As you know yourself, you can go to a party with a swollen ankle or take a trip even though you have a headache because your enthusiasm for what you are doing carries you in spite of these minor difficulties. However, at this period in your life, you find there is nothing you really want to do, and you need as much help as you can get from your body in order to make yourself get through each day. Have a thorough physical examination. Sometimes the experience of grief itself starts problems. If you find there are any, do whatever your doctor suggests. If you don't have any, be grateful and carry on. I know of a bereaved man who also went to a psychiatrist for the same reason that he would go to a doctor, to see if he had a clean bill of mental health.

One last question is that of travel. Early in grief the only visit that is helpful for you is one to a friend or relative who is close to you and who realizes that you may often be absorbed in your own grief. Visits to other people should wait until later. You would not be a good guest, because of your temporary self-centered involvement, and you should not have to keep social engagements which might serve only as distractions. Extensive trips are not helpful either, because you carry your sorrow with you. No matter how new and strange each sight might be, interest is in the eye of the beholder, and you will have little to invest in anything outside yourself for a while. You need old friends near you at this time; few strangers are going to be interested in your problems. So, save travel for a later time when your emotions are free to enjoy the people you visit and the new experiences you have.

There are many other practical problems which you must solve, and they vary from person to person. Only the basic application to the most common ones has been discussed. The key to making such decisions is to go slowly. Try to avoid making important ones when you are still upset by grief; and, on the other hand, do not let decisions and their activities interfere with your work of mourning. However, do not prolong mourning beyond the time when you become aware of your own readiness for experience outside yourself.

By this time you are familiar enough with the psychology of grief to apply it yourself to whatever new situations arise as you work through the second phase of mourning.

7

Is Preparation for Bereavement Possible?

NO ONE IS EVER READY to face the separation of death, particularly the death of someone still healthy and vital. But if there is anything like preventive medicine, it is preventive strength which is built up long before the emergency in which it is needed. In a sense, you prepare throughout your life for the adjustments you must make when you go through a bereavement.

For those who believe, a major source of strength is your own religious faith. However, religious beliefs vary so that they cannot be discussed in general. The great differences between beliefs also means that someone in your particular church is the chief source outside yourself who can supplement you spiritually at the time of a bereavement—who can support you as only someone with your beliefs is able to.

A second strength, which may or may not be associated with religion, is the development of a purpose in life that is not centered on any one person.

A moving illustration of the way such a purpose operates is given in *Man's Search for Meaning* by Viktor Frankl, a well-known Viennese psychiatrist. In it he shows that the one indispensable factor needed to meet any problem lies within the individual himself. The little book describes Dr. Frankl's years in a prison camp, when he was stripped of every support ordinarily required by men. Dr. Frankl did not know whether his wife, whom he deeply loved, was alive or dead; his daily life was filled with demeaning work and meaningless cruelty; he had barely enough food and sleep to keep him alive; many of his fellow prisoners became dehumanized animals; and over this whole desolate picture lay the unnerving question of how long such an existence would have to be endured or whether it would end at all should the enemy win the war.

Long before Dr. Frankl was put into the prison camp, he had unknowingly prepared for even so demoralizing an experience as the one he had to go through. He believes that the most important task that each person has is to find a meaning for life, a meaning that is reflected in all choices that he has to make. His own search for meaning created within him a purpose so strong that it sustained him through his years in prison. The only choice he could make had to do with his ultimate purpose, since he had no choice of occupation, circumstances of living, or companionship. His purpose, that of writing a book, was so important to him that he emerged from this experience a whole person, strengthened rather than destroyed by the horror and depersonalization imposed on him.

Before you can get through your grief, you, too, will have to find a meaning in life not associated with the person you have lost. This will require growth, very painful growth on your part. You would, of course, prefer to have been left in your cocoon of personal contentment. But you have no choice, just as Dr. Frankl had no choice, in the circumstance of life to be faced.

A third inner strength is your own emotional maturity. If you have had everything you wanted when you wanted it, you will have trouble at the time of the irreversible deprivation of death. If you have not been sure of yourself in meeting new experiences, this, too, will be reflected in the way you meet the new experience of grief. If you have a healthy and confident attitude toward problems, you have developed your own best preventive therapy for meeting grief. So the emotional tone of your life style either impedes or helps you in meeting grief.

The tragic story of a woman who could not face reality illustrates the way "life style" is reflected in facing grief. She was a charming woman, but she had a weakness recognized by her immediate family. If faced with a disagreeable reality, she suffered intensely. They shielded her as often as they could. Her husband had to have an operation and confided in his son, who took him to the hospital—the son called his mother late in the afternoon to tell her about the operation after all had gone well. When a daughter who lived in another part of the country was going to have a baby, the family agreed that her mother should not know about it until later, although the daughter had visited home when she was three months pregnant.

When the mother was in her sixties, her husband had to have another operation. Instead of correcting the problem suspected, the operation disclosed that he had a cancer. It had gone so far that nothing could be done for him. His wife could not believe the diagnosis and would not allow the doctors to tell it to her husband. Nine months followed in which she continued to hope, although he painfully and steadily deteriorated with each day. He died in his own room, and she insisted that he be embalmed there. He was then laid in his bed, and for three days she was comforted, for he seemed to be himself in his own place.

He was finally placed in his coffin. She managed to get through the funeral, but in the following months she could not come out of her depression. Six months later she died of a heart attack. Her life style operated painfully as she faced the final problem of her husband's illness and death, which she could not be spared.

Another woman had always met problems with reality and vigor. Her husband died when she was forty. Her first Christmas without him she took her three teenage children skiing instead of going through the "usual" Christmas at home with both sets of grandparents. She knew Christmas would never be "usual" again. She got a masters degree. And when the two older children were in college, she found a teaching position in a university in another state and moved there with her teen-age son. There was an air of expectancy about her, and she planned a future that had no limits. She sometimes referred to her life with her husband, the fun they had, the house they loved, the friends they partied with and the crazy things they all did together. She appreciated the good life she had had and looked back on it with love and nostalgia. But she became thoroughly involved in making a completely different kind of good life and threw her whole being into what she was doing.

Few people meet rebuilding a life with this woman's verve. But if you have been emotionally mature in meeting other kinds of day-to-day problems, you have already developed an approach that will help you meet a serious life adjustment like bereavement.

There is a last strength that is needed in bereavement. This one can be developed in a relatively short time, for it is an understanding of the psychology of grief discussed in this book. This specialized knowledge can help you to understand your own emotions and hence avoid the problems of poorly resolved grief, which can make the traumatic experience of grief even more difficult than it need be.

These four strengths are also important

in the adjustment of people who are divorced or who have experienced a major physical or emotional loss. Such people certainly need spiritual strength, purpose, emotional maturity, and they must also make the same adjustments that those in grief go through, the same breaking away from a past life, and the same developing of ties to a new one. Beyond these similarities, however, there are many differences —differences even between the needs of the divorced and of those who have suffered a major physical loss.

Our society takes it for granted that we will provide financial protection for our families. But we think little of providing the spiritual and emotional protection developed through these four strengths; yet the help they give is indispensable and much more durable than that given by money.

8

Problems of Certain Groups of People

MANY PEOPLE must find their way through the sorrow and loneliness of mourning. However, there are several groups whose problems are so common that they deserve discussion. The problems of some of these can only be presented; there are no solutions. For others, solutions are suggested.

Every man or woman who has been married and has lost his mate knows what it means to suddenly lose the expression of sex, its shared intimacy and release, and, less obviously, its daily reminders that each belongs to another. Once, to my surprise, a widowed matron I had always thought of as rather formal and distant said, "But there's no one now to tweak my nose." And I added to myself, "Or pat my knee, circle my waist, or ruffle my hair," whatever the casual way of making vital physical contact might have been. The cry of a dignified man whose wife had died was that he would never again be "Lad" to another. A close friend wept knowing that no one would suddenly enfold her tenderly, roughly, or any other way. After Albert's death even Queen Victoria echoed this universal cry when she wondered who would then call her Victoria. A whole area of personality—gentle, exciting, even playful—is now denied. Probably never again will you be "first" with another.

Any bereavement is hard to bear, but the bereavement of women poses special problems. People who have little change in a life pattern seem to make an easier adjustment to grief than those whose lives are dislocated. A bereaved woman, more often than a man, must make major changes in her life. She may have to accept a lower standard of living because her income is reduced. This may mean moving to a less attractive or smaller home; changing neighborhoods; economizing at every turn; taking a job; worrying about leaving children with someone else to care for; giving up contact with the friends she saw chiefly during the day. All this is difficult enough to do in itself, without simultaneously experiencing the adjustment of mourning.

If a woman has lost a husband, she soon finds that she has been living in a world where couples form the basis of most social life. The extra man is in great demand, but the extra woman is merely an addition to the growing number of single women. A man knows he can find a woman, or perhaps several, as company if he chooses. He can even select from this wide variety of women should he feel he wants to remarry. But a woman's perspective has no such freedom of choice or security of outlook.

A woman usually knows little about handling investments, insurance, and property, and yet she may suddenly have to make important decisions related to them.

Something quite subtle happens to a woman psychologically when she is widowed. When she needs most to be a follower, she must assume initiative, not only in business but in taking charge of her whole life. When she does this, she is violating something feminine within her. She is assuming a leadership role that is thrust upon her. But she violates her femininity with less bewilderment if she recognizes exactly what she is doing, if she understands why she hesitates to do what she must do as she fights her way through her bereavement.

It is a man's world in many ways important to daily life—social, business, and psychological. A woman may learn to deal with business, but her social role is rooted in our mores, and her psychological role is rooted within her own nature.

Men have problems during mourning also. Their chief one stems from the training they have had not to cry. Since childhood, they have been told, "Be brave. Don't cry." Men bottle up their grief because they feel that tears are not masculine. Dr. Erich Lindemann, who observed many bereaved people who were hospitalized after fire had killed family members, found that men in grief held themselves tense and were unable to relax for fear that they might break down. But when a man can cry, there is great relief from the released emotions. A police officer, certainly a symbol of masculinity in our society, told me that for months following the death of their son in Vietnam he went downstairs each morning and "bawled" where he would not upset his wife with his tears. He said he was sure that he could not have gotten through each day without this release. One reason for crying, an unconscious one, is to return to the weakness of childhood when little ones cry out for help. Of course, women fit more naturally into this dependent, helpless role than do men.

A mature and perceptive man wrote openly to a friend of his feelings when his wife died. "I would have given the world for ten minutes longer. So ends our forty years together, and the emptiness of the house and futility of all the things one goes on doing appalls me." In a later letter he said, "The first weeks alone were hell. There were times when I thought I'd never get through them. Being alone made it possible to let myself go." Here the implication is that he needed to keep up for society but was relieved to be able to let down and cry when by himself.

He continued, "I live in a curious state almost of well being, except that at intervals, without warning, reality steps in and I am undone. And one has a curious sense of guilt, too, that one even goes on surviving. I suppose everyone feels that way.

"I am ridiculously busy, looking after myself, tidying the house, doing the shopping on weekends, doing my laundry, cooking, so that I am outrageously tired, though I sleep badly."

Mourning is a time in the life of a man when it is normal to behave in a way that may seem abnormal. Men who repress their grief and who do not cry, not only experience almost unbearable tension but they risk slowing up or impeding their recovery. Less self-conscious societies than ours often show more wisdom about human behavior than we do. An old Mexican saying, "Sorrow, like the river, must be given vent lest it erode the bank," suggests the wisdom of crying.

Children compose a third group that has special problems at the time of death. What to tell them about death is an individual matter because the needs of each child and his relationship to the people around him vary so. However, there are principles that can serve as a guide. It is not only important to get a child through the immediate situation, but it is important to do this in a way that will help him in the future with this and other problems.

There was a time when birth and death were a part of everyday life on farms and in small towns. Now they are more removed from our experience and consequently are harder to explain. Yet there are still opportunities to deal with death honestly and helpfully.

I was visiting a family for a few days, and when I arrived there was talk about the pet kitten, which was not eating much and seemed listless. Then one morning six-year-old Sally came running in to the house with the kitten dead in her arms. Her mother held it lovingly in her lap as she comforted Sally. Then she began to talk about how the kitten was sicker than they had all thought; how she wouldn't drink her milk at all now because she no longer needed it to feed her body; how the kitten couldn't feel anything because her little body was dead. Sally gradually stopped crying as she listened to the wonder of the things her mother was telling her, as she began to understand something of the mystery of death. I can see Sally now as she stood at the telephone trying hard to explain to her best friend that "Fluffy Ruffles had died because she was too sick to live." That afternoon the two children had a backyard funeral. The kitten lay on a soft cloth crumpled up in a shoe box. The girls carefully and lovingly decorated the grave with a headstone and some flowers from the garden. How much Sally had learned about death that one day. She had been close to the changes death can bring, she had gone through the ritual of burial, and, most important, she had experienced the finality of death. After Sally had gone to bed, her parents talked about getting her a new kitten. But they finally decided not to because they felt she would learn only that everything could be made right by all-powerful parents and that one affection can be easily replaced by another. They concluded that only later after she had gotten over the loss of the kitten would she be ready to have another pet.

Children should not only have the right to grieve, but they should also have the chance to relate death to experiences in their own lives. A mother who says, "Jimmy's going to miss his grandmother, isn't he?" or "You will certainly be sorry not to play with Bobby's soldier uncle any more" is opening up the opportunity to talk about the loneliness death can bring into life.

When there has been a death in the child's own home, he senses that something of great importance is going on, and if he is not told anything about it, he feels excluded and alone. A child should not be a part of all the activities and traumas surrounding death. Neither should he be taken off to a friend's home until the funeral is over, then returned to his own home, where, for example, the mother died suddenly. The young child thinks, "I had fun while I was gone. But I missed Mommy and Daddy. But where is Mommy? What do they mean, she's in Heaven? Gone away? What did I do that made her leave me? Doesn't she love me? Why didn't she take me, too? Who will take care of me? Everybody's so strange and quiet. Why does Granny cry? There are flowers around. They're pretty. A lot of people are visiting us. I'm hungry and want my lunch. Why doesn't Granny stop talking to the people and get me some lunch. They're talking about Mommy. Where *is* Mommy? I'm tired of playing with my blocks. Where's Mommy?"

This confusion is natural. If the father in this example is not able to talk to the child about the death, someone he is used to and feels close to should tell him gently as much as he is old enough to understand about what happened. Usually such a person is a woman. A child may have strange ideas about death if he is not helped to understand it in this first talk.

Authorities believe that he should be told the truth. After the death of a mother, for example, *a child should be told that Mommy died,* difficult as that may be to do. Then all that the child asks should be answered. If the child is told that "Mommy went away," he may realistically ask, "Where has she gone?" "When is she coming back?" Euphemisms like "gone away" are hard for a child to understand because he takes them literally. He may wait, daily expecting Mommy's return.

He should be told also that Mommy loved him very much, rather than allow him to wonder why she deserted him. He should be told that Mommy was very sick and that is why she could not live, that Mommy knew how much he loved her, rather than the child's thinking that the death was somehow his fault. He should be told that people usually die when they are older, rather than fear his own death. One little boy reflected this fear when he asked, "Am I old enough to die?" He should be assured he is going to be cared for by others in his family, now and always. Here a kiss and hug are more comfort than the actual words. This long, difficult conversation is best carried on with the child held close by the comforter if the child wants this physical contact.

If, in this first talk, these ideas are worked in somehow, the most typical fears of a child will have been anticipated before he has a chance to imagine and magnify them. Whoever talks to the child must feel the way and be guided by the child's responses and questions.

If the father, for example, is able to talk with the child, then the comfort of the strongest substitute for Mommy is right there. But the parent may not always be home to talk with him in the days ahead, so it is wise to share part of this first talk with the friend or relative who is going to be caring for him. The child needs someone who will always be there in order to answer any questions, talk about Mommy, and, most important, understand how he feels. The woman who is taking care of him should give his questions simple but honest answers. However, sharing honest emotions is of even greater importance. Tears might naturally well up in her eyes as she reflects his feeling. "I know how you miss Mommy. I miss her too and wish she were here right now." She may suggest his feelings throughout the day. "I know you wish Mommy could give you your milk." "You miss Mommy at nap time." This should continue only as long as the child really seems to need this help. If the child is able to bring his feelings and thoughts out into the open, a vital step will have been taken in resolving his grief. He will be able to do this most easily if someone is with him who is responsive and reassuring.

One other important thing about little children is that they are centered in the present, and their own immediate satisfactions are naturally important to them. When a child's life has been disrupted by a death, it is important to maintain his daily schedule. His routine should be kept so that he feels supported and secure, at least in that area of his life. The household is sure to be busy with the unusual activities and conversations that surround a death. So it perhaps would be wise to take a child to a friend's for a part of each day until his home is more like the place he is used to.

Stability is also important for older children. A familiar home can help the adjustment to a loss. I know a woman whose husband died when their son was a sophomore in high school. Although it was financially hard for her to keep their home, she stayed there until he went to college and then sold it.

Children always need the support of relationships that are loving and honest. But there is no time when this is more important than during a bereavement. A child should feel that there is someone constantly near who understands his feelings, and it is even more comforting if that person shares them.

There is always the question of whether to take children to the funeral. It is generally agreed that the answer depends altogether upon the individual circumstances. Small children are naturally disturbing at a funeral and so little aware of what is going on that it usually does not seem wise to take them. Older children themselves may have a strong preference about going or not going. If they do go to a funeral, they should be told what to expect at both the service and burial. Children who are used to going to church with their parents would find a funeral where there is no casket little different in form from a regular service so this kind of funeral should present no problem.

When children ask about the casket, the grave, and the cemetery, their questions deserve honest answers with as much detail as each child demands.

If a child's grief is persistent and long lasting, professional help should be found through a doctor, minister, principal, or anyone who has earned the confidence and respect of the family and who is in a position to know about special counseling resources.

Although it is sometimes hard for a family to accept the short time that it usually takes a child to recover from grief, his return to normal should be recognized gratefully if he seems genuinely involved in his activities and is not using them as a distraction. The continuing grief of others should not be imposed on children when they have adjusted to the loss. As time goes on, references to the person who has died should be natural and a part of the talk about the life once shared. For the child, the death and the grief that went with it become gradually absorbed in his own demanding and exciting present.

9

The Third Phase of Mourning

"WHAT CAN I DO?" asked a friend whose husband had died. "There's nothing, absolutely nothing that I even want to do." Each person must take stock of the special resources he has within himself. He will find, of course, that they are the very ones he has spent a lifetime building.

A teacher had each of his students spend four hours alone in the wilderness, Thoreau-fashion. One matter-of-fact boy returned from his lonely adventure bored, and the teacher said, "Look to yourself to see why. You were your only companion." So each of us must look to himself.

Some people return to old interests and develop them further. Some find new ones. Most of us do both. In fact, this trying out of interests goes on side by side with the other experiences of grief described in the second phase of mourning.

Whatever filled the crevices of a complete personal life before a loss may not be as satisfying after one. Activity for activity's sake is not a panacea, any more than the mere passing of time is.

Those people who have work to turn to are the fortunate ones. It can be a great sustainer, especially if it is personally satisfying. A friend who was suffering because of a death said to me over and over, "You have your work to go to every day. But my days are so long. They have no focus!" Many people already have work. Some women who do not, may take jobs reluctantly, resentfully, half-heartedly, and end by losing themselves in them, for mourning, as well as other frustrating experiences, may bring out people's latent creative abilities.

Those who need not work to earn a living may need to work to make a life. They can surely find volunteer work in a world that has as many needs as ours has. But volunteer work has one great danger. There is no penalty for slacking—no penalty except to the person who is cheating himself out of release from self-centeredness.

The family is a most important resource, but it usually supplements a life, and is not the center for it. Friends, of course, are an asset; however, a few true friends are worth a legion of the casual variety. The list of individual interests is endless and unique to each person. A book on the subject of what women can do is *Women Alone* by Isabella Taves.

Some people go back to school to prepare for a job, develop a skill, or enlarge an interest. Going to school is an excellent way to enter into a new life and meet new people.

It is not important to discuss in detail the many ramifications of what such a new life might bring. Having successfully freed your emotions during the little understood second phase of mourning, you are ready to carry on on your own and follow whatever new pattern your life takes in the third phase.

There are three warnings about building a new life. First, each person's interests must be truly his own. Because there is often an insatiable appetite for any substitute that is not real, people need to be careful not to fool themselves about the honest worth of interests. The only enduring ones are those which use to the fullest whatever special abilities each person has. Any time or talent once spent in behalf of the person no longer living must eventually be given to other interests. Being honest is insurance against building a new life on a shoddy foundation that cannot bear the weight of the years ahead. Finding real interests may take some experimenting, but eventually some are sure to develop that are worth investing life in. But they must be truly fulfilling and not merely fill time.

Second, anyone who has rebuilt a life knows that it costs great effort. The bereaved, the divorced, as well as those who suffer a major physical disability know this lesson well—too well. All day, every moment, such a person must make an effort—dressing, eating, walking, working—every common daily experience is different and difficult. It takes time and determination to rebuild an entirely new life pattern. The first gestures toward involvement are almost certain to be artificial and forced. But priming the pump is important. There *must* be a beginning. C. S. Lewis says, "No one ever told me about the laziness of grief. . . . I loathe the slightest effort." But each person who grieves must make that effort or rot.

In the January, 1968, issue of *Reader's Digest,* an article about Einstein mentions his experience with grief which puts this principle of involvement to work.

> When his wife died he was deeply shaken, but insisted that now more than ever was the time to be working hard. I vividly remember going to his house to work with him during that sad time. His face was haggard and grief-lined, but he put forth a great effort to concentrate. Seeking to help him, I steered the discussion away from routine matters into more diffi-

cult theoretical problems, and Einstein gradually became absorbed in the discussion. We kept at it for some two hours, and at the end his eyes were no longer sad. As I left, he thanked me with moving sincerity, but the words he found sounded almost incongruous. "It was fun," he said. He had had a moment of surcease from grief, and these groping words expressed a deep emotion.

Third, an individual timing is involved in letting grief find its course and allowing a new way of living gradually to take over. This slow process cannot be hurried. But inner needs must eventually give way to the world of reality outside the self.

I knew two women who were bereaved at about the same time. Each was deeply hurt and completely lost. They allowed the suffering of grief to have its slow way. They did not avoid it with drugs or drink. They experienced grief without camouflage. Yet one of them was able to open up to life sooner than the other. Once in a while, life returned her effort with a small dividend earned from a new interest that brought genuine satisfaction which didn't have to be *pretended.* Such satisfactions began to come more frequently; they accumulated a momentum of their own that helped carry her life without the constant effort of hollow acting. These lengthening periods of feeling better were like relief from severe pain. When I heard her burst out in a hearty laugh, I knew that she was on her way to healing.

The other woman did not find this kind of satisfaction until months later. There can be no hurrying this process. A graphic comparison is the lifting of a scab when it is ready to come off. If it is lifted too soon, it tears the flesh. And so with the emotions of one who grieves—they cannot be pushed too fast. Of course there's a scar—one created by the depth of grief and the stretch of growth. But a scar need not incapacitate.

10

Conclusion

YOU HAVE GRIEVED and so have come through a deep experience—not an experience you wanted, but one that has created in you a new self. Nietzsche said, "That which does not kill me makes me stronger." When you first knew grief, you felt you could not live through it. But a great stress such as grief forces growth, and it is this growth that develops the strength you didn't know you had.

But growth of what? Greater personal adequacy, greater wholeness. You have also had to stretch to the fullest every resource of spirit and emotion. Doing this, you found a part of yourself you might never have known, and this makes you realize how far below your potential you have always lived. You have underestimated what to expect of yourself. No wonder you are no longer the same person.

It was Nietzsche again who declared, "No one can draw more out of things, books included, than he already knows." Think back then on what you already know; think back on your own sequence of growth as it has unfolded. You will recognize changes in several areas.

You probably have greater ability to meet adversity—a new strength within you makes you confident of this.

In addition, scientists have found that suffering releases creative abilities and talents in fields such as art and writing.

According to Proust, "Grief develops the power of the mind," and he could have added, "and the heart." You may really feel, perhaps for the first time, the hurt of the braced legs that want to dance and the eyes that cannot see. You have gained a greater kinship with the total human effort.

One other asset may be your growing need to contribute to the eternal stream of goodness in the world that has always represented man's best impulses. This can be drive and direction enough to carry a lifetime. It served very well for Jesus of Nazareth.

Most important, you may have found strength in your religion that you didn't realize was there until you put it to the test.

Realizing that some of these new strengths are yours, you can never again return to your former life. You can be no less than the self you have now become. Much as you wished to avoid this growth, you had no choice in the circumstance that forced it on you. But you did have a choice in the way you met that painful circumstance, either in tragedy that ended your life or in growth that gave it a new beginning.

Bibliography

Abraham, Karl. Selected Papers. London: Hogarth Press, 1927.

Anderson, Charles. "Aspects of Pathological Grief and Mourning." *International Journal of Psycho-analysis* 30: 48-55.

Arnstein, Helene S. *What to Tell Your Child.* New York, Pocket Books, 1964.

Becker, Diane, and Margolin, Faith. "How Surviving Parents Handled Their Children's Adaptation to the Crisis of Loss." *American Journal of Psychiatry* 37: 753-57.

Bowlby, John. "Processes of Mourning." *The International Journal of Psychoanalysis* 42: 317-40.

Camus, Albert. *The Plague.* New York: Alfred A. Knopf, 1948.

Cornell, George W. Column in Fort Collins (Colo.) *Coloradoan,* March 23, 1969.

Engel, George. "Is Grief a Disease?" *Psychosomatic Medicine* 23: 18-22.

Fishman, Katherine Davis. "Death in the Family." Denver *Post,* February 11, 1969, p. 63.

Frankl, Viktor. *Man's Search for Meaning.* New York: Washington Square Press, 1963.

Freud, Sigmund. "Mourning and Melancholia." *Collected Papers,* Vol. 4. London: Hogarth Press, 1950.

Gorer, Geoffrey. *Death, Grief and Mourning.* Garden City: Doubleday and Co., 1965.

Gunther, John. *Death Be Not Proud.* New York: Harper, 1949.

Heilbrunn, Gert. "On Weeping." *Psychoanalytic Quarterly* 24: 245.

Hoffman, Banesh. "The Unforgettable Albert Einstein." *The Reader's Digest,* January 1968, p. 109.

Howells, William Dean. *The Rise of Silas Lapham.* New York: New American Library, 1963.

Jackson, Edgar. *Understanding Grief.* New York: Abingdon Press, 1957.

Jacobson, Edith. "Normal and Pathological Moods: Their Nature and Function." *Psychoanalytic Study of the Child* 12: 73-113.

Klein, Melanie. "Mourning and Its Relation to Manic-depressive States." *International Journal of Psycho-analysis* 21: 125-53.

Lewis, C. S. *A Grief Observed.* New York: Seabury Press, 1961.

Liebman, Joshua. *Peace of Mind.* New

York: Simon and Schuster, 1946.
Lindemann, Erich. "Symptomatology and Management of Acute Grief." *American Journal of Psychiatry* 51: 141-48.
McNeil, Elton. *Human Socialization.* Belmont, Cal.: Brooks/Cole Publishing Co., 1969.
Marshall, Catherine. *To Live Again.* New York: McGraw-Hill Book Co., 1957.
Parkes, Colin Murray. "Bereavement Reactions." *British Journal of Medical Psychology* (1965), pp. 13-26.
Rogers, Carl. *On Becoming a Person.* Boston: Houghton-Mifflin, 1961.
Tausk, L. E. "Compensation As a Means of Discounting the Motive of Depression." *International Journal of Psycho-analysis* 5: 130-40.
Taves, Isabella. *Women Alone.* New York: Funk and Wagnall, 1968.
Tournier, Paul. *The Meaning of Persons.* New York: Harper, 1957.